Bargain Toronto

*A Guide to over 100 Warehouse
Sales and Warehouse Outlets
in Metro Toronto*

Bargain Toronto

*A Guide to over 100 Warehouse
Sales and Warehouse Outlets
in Metro Toronto*

Sandra Hargreaves

Whitecap Books
Vancouver / Toronto

Edited by Linda Ostrowalker
Cover and interior design by Carolyn Deby

Typeset at Vancouver Desktop Publishing, Vancouver
Printed and bound in Canada by Friesen Printers, Altona,
Manitoba

Canadian Cataloguing in Publication Data
Hargreaves, Sandra.
    Bargain Toronto

    ISBN 1-55110-026-6

    1. Shopping—Ontario—Toronto—Guide-books.
    2. Outlet stores—Ontario—Toronto—Guide-books.
    3. Toronto (Ont.)—Description—Guide-books.
I. Title.
TX337.C22T65 1992   380.1'45'0009713541   C92-091023-8

TABLE OF CONTENTS

♣

INTRODUCTION

As the excessive eighties have given way to the nervous nineties it has become fashionable to search out the best "deal." No longer is paying top dollar for a product the thing to do—gone are the days of excessive consumerism. Now it is chic to buy at the best price possible.

Searching for a "deal" does not necessarily mean giving up all those little luxuries such as designer clothes, bone china, or brand name luggage. It just means that shoppers have to get a little smarter and know where to find the best bargains. Many people think heading south to the United States is the answer to great bargain hunting. But why subject yourself to the aggravations of cross-border shopping, which may involve long line-ups at customs and major mathematical calculations to figure out the exchange rate, when some of the best buys are right here in Toronto?

In order to make the most of these great buys the smart shopper only needs two things—a knowledge of the regular retail price and a copy of this book!

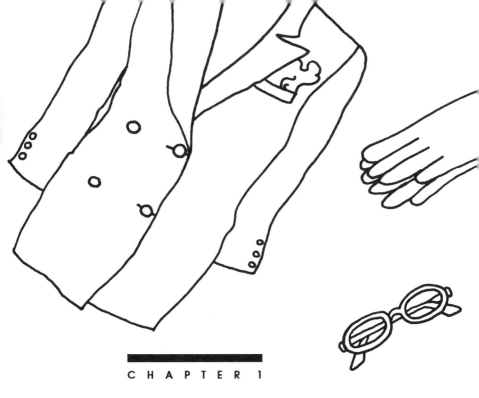

C H A P T E R 1

Clearance Centres and Manufacturers' Outlets

The vogue in retailing seems to be a move to opening stores and calling them "discount outlets" even though the products offered have never had a previous retail price. As the recession bites deeper and retailers offer higher discounts it becomes more difficult to identify true bargain centres. In this chapter I have included three types of outlets: "bona fide" clearance centres where the majority of the stock has been cleared from other stores, usually to make way for the arrival of a new season's inventory; manufacturers' stores that are based at the manufacturing plant or head office of the company; and outlets that I believe offer prices which are significantly lower than regular retail.

Before going to one of these outlets it is wise to check the regular retail price as some items may not be offered at any great saving. Although I have taken great care to be accurate, please check with the individual stores to confirm hours of operation and payment particulars. Also, in this volatile retail environment, it is a good idea to ensure the outlet is still open before driving long distances.

The first part of this chapter is arranged by product type and gives all the relevant details of the outlet's operation. Then, for ease of use, outlets are listed by geographical area.

Where You'll Find the Best Bargains

C L O T H I N G

Menswear

Crawford and Co.

* Lawrence Plaza (Lawrence and Bathurst)
  Phone: 782-8137

  Monday to Friday 10:00 a.m.–9:00 p.m.,
  Saturday 10:00 a.m.–6:00 p.m.
  Visa/MasterCard

Men's and boys' clothing at discounted prices.
Everything is discounted to some extent but
higher discounts can be found as seasons
change. Usually 30% off but can be as high as
70% off regular retail.

International Clothiers

* 111 Orfus Road (north of Lawrence and west
  of Dufferin)
  Phone: 785-1733

  Monday to Friday 10:00 a.m.–9:00 p.m.,
  Saturday 10:00 a.m.–6:00 p.m.
  Visa/MasterCard/Amex

Men's suits, jackets, trench coats, and pants at
20%–60% savings.

Le Club

- 720 King Street West, Suite 215 (King and Bathurst)
Phone: 947-1041

  Monday to Saturday 10:00 a.m.–6:30 p.m.
  Visa/MasterCard

  Imported Italian men's suits at 30%–40% off regular retail.

Royal Shirt Company Ltd.

- 40 Adesso Drive, Concord (Steeles and Highway 400)
Phone: 738-4676

  Monday to Wednesday 9:00 a.m.–6:00 p.m.,
  Thursday/Friday 9:00 a.m.–9:00 p.m.,
  Saturday 10:00 a.m.–5:00 p.m.
  Visa

  Dress and sports shirts on sale all year round but the best deals are found at the semi-annual sales (usually in December and June) when there can be savings of up to 75%.

Shiffer Hillman

- 2700 Dufferin Street, Unit 3 (Dufferin, north of Eglinton)
Phone: 787-5688

  Monday to Saturday 9:00 a.m.–6:00 p.m.
  Visa/MasterCard

  Men's suits, jackets, slacks, and coats plus made-to-measure at 30%–50% off comparable retail prices.

Tip Top Tailors Warehouse Outlet

- Dixie Value Mall, 1250 South Service Road, Mississauga (Q.E.W. and South Dixie Road)
Phone: 274-0114

  Monday to Friday 9:30 a.m.–9:00 p.m., Saturday 9:30 a.m.–6:00 p.m. Visa/MasterCard

Clearance outlet for other Tip Top stores. Can be savings of up to 70% on men's suits, pants, and jackets.

Ladieswear

Braemar and Braemar Petites

- Eaton Sheridan Place, 2225 Erin Mills Parkway, Mississauga (off Q.E.W.)
Phone: 855-1270

- Woodbine Centre (Rexdale Boulevard and Highway 27)
Phone: 674-5595

  Monday to Friday 10:00 a.m.–9:00 p.m., Saturday 10:00 a.m.–6:00 p.m. Visa/MasterCard

Clearance centres for Toronto area stores. Up to 70% off on end-of-season stock plus some special purchases.

Dan Howard's Maternity Factory Outlet

- 257 Dundas Street E. (Dundas between Cawthra and Highway 10)
Phone: 846-6776

- 300 Steeles Avenue W., Thornhill (2 blocks west of Yonge)
  Phone: 731-6177

  Monday and Thursday 10:00 a.m.–9:00 p.m.,
  Tuesday/Wednesday/
  Friday/Saturday 10:00 a.m.–6:00 p.m.
  Visa/MasterCard

  25%–65% off top quality maternity clothing.

Fairweather

- Rexdale Plaza, 2267 Islington Avenue (Highway 401 and Islington N.)
  Phone: 743-1706

  Monday to Friday 10:00 a.m.–9:00 p.m.,
  Saturday 9:30 a.m.–6:00 p.m.
  Visa/MasterCard

  Up to 50% off on clearance merchandise from other stores in Toronto area. Some regular merchandise is also carried.

Finds

- 365 Jane Street (north of Bloor)
  Phone: 761-9613

  Monday to Friday 10:00 a.m.–7:00 p.m.,
  Saturday 10:00 a.m.–6:00 p.m.
  Visa/MasterCard

  Discounted ladies' designer clothes. Save 50%–70% on higher end ladieswear. No connection to "Finds" which is Lipton's and Heritage House.

Finds

* Cumberland Terrace (Bay and Cumberland)
  Phone: 968-6520

  Monday to Wednesday 10:00 a.m.–6:00 p.m.,
  Thursday/Friday 10:00 a.m.–8:00 p.m.,
  Saturday 10:00 a.m.–6:00 p.m.

* 2 Steeles Avenue W. (Yonge and Steeles)
  Phone: 886-2516

  Monday to Saturday 10:00 a.m.–6:00 p.m.,
  Thursday, 10:00 a.m.–9:00 p.m.
  Visa/MasterCard

Clearance centres for the Lipton's and Heritage
House chains.

Glenayr Kitten Factory Outlet

* 100 Thorncliffe Park Drive (Thorncliffe Park
  and Overlea Boulevard)
  Phone: 421-3280

  Tuesday to Saturday 9:30 a.m.–4:30 p.m.
  Visa/MasterCard

Direct-from-the-manufacturer ladies'
sportswear and sweaters.

United Factory Outlet

* 450 Alliance Avenue (Jane, south of
  Eglinton)
  Phone: 769-1234

  Monday to Friday 11:30 a.m.–3:30 p.m.
  Visa/MasterCard

Ladies' sweaters, skirts, and jackets plus some
children's wear.

Ladies' and Men's Clothing

Forsyth Factory Outlet

- 1825 Dundas Street E., Mississauga
  (Dundas, west of Highway 427)
  Phone: 625-5073

  *Tuesday/Wednesday 11:00 a.m.–5:00 p.m.,
  Thursday/Friday 11:00 a.m.–6:00 p.m.,
  Saturday 10:00 a.m.–5:00 p.m.
  Visa/MasterCard*

Up to 75% off ladies' and men's designer clothing including Pierre Cardin, Manhattan, and Lady Forsyth.

Hardy Amies Factory Outlet

- 32 Mendota Road (east of Royal York, north of The Queensway)
  Phone: 251-3114

  *Friday only 9:30 a.m.–2:30 p.m.
  Cash*

Men's and women's shirts—first quality and seconds. Note: No returns and no facilities for trying clothes on.

Heritage Fine Clothing

- 103 Orfus Road (north of Lawrence and west of Dufferin)
  Phone: 789-5192

  *Monday to Friday 9:00 a.m.–9:00 p.m.,
  Saturday 9:00 a.m.–6:00 p.m.
  Visa/MasterCard/Amex*

Men's and ladies' coats, suits, and jackets at considerable discounts.

Holt Renfrew Last Call

* 370 Steeles Avenue W. (between Yonge and
  Bathurst)
  Phone: 886-7444

  Monday to Friday 10:00 a.m.–9:00 p.m.,
  Saturday 10:00 a.m.–6:00 p.m.
  Visa/MasterCard/Amex

Clearance centre for Holt Renfrew chain.
Discounts of 50%–75% off regular retail prices.
Frequent special sales to clear end-of-season
ladies' and men's fashions.

Le Chateau Depot

* 2056 Danforth Avenue (Danforth and
  Woodbine)
  Phone: 421-2822

  Monday to Friday 10:00 a.m.–9:00 p.m.,
  Saturday 9:30 a.m.–6:00 p.m.
  Visa/MasterCard/Amex

Up to 50% off ladies' and men's clothing being
cleared from the Le Chateau chain.

Marks and Spencer Clearance Store

* 3003 Danforth Avenue
  (Danforth and Victoria Park)
  Phone: 698-1669

  Monday/Tuesday 10:00 a.m.–7:00 p.m.,
  Wednesday/Thursday/Friday
  10:00 a.m.– 9:00 p.m.
  Saturday 9:30 a.m.–6:00 p.m.
  Visa/MasterCard

End-of-line men's, ladies', and children's wear
at 20%–50% off retail plus one-off samples and

special purchases. Very little underwear,
mostly outer wear.

Parkhurst Factory Store

* 20 Research Road (Brentcliffe, south of
  Eglinton)
  Phone: 421-3773 ext. 140

  *Monday to Saturday 10:00 a.m.–4:00 p.m.,
  Wednesday/Thursday 10:00 a.m.–8:00 p.m.
  Visa/MasterCard*

Up to 50% off knitted sweaters, skirts, and
accessories (hats, gloves, and scarves). Fall and
spring sales to clear discontinued lines and
samples.

Stitches Warehouse Outlet

* Dixie Value Mall, 1250 South Service Road,
  Mississauga (Q.E.W. and South Dixie Road)
  Phone: 271-1400

  *Monday to Friday 9:30 a.m.–9:00 p.m.,
  Saturday 9:30 a.m.–6:00 p.m.
  Visa/MasterCard*

From 30%–50% off ladies' and men's leathers,
shirts, and jackets being cleared from Stitches
stores. Some special purchases made for this
store.

Winners

* Lawrence Plaza (Bathurst and Lawrence)
  Phone: 782-4469

* Thornhill Square (Bayview and John)
  Phone: 731-3201

- Dixie Value Mall (Q.E.W. and South Dixie Road)
  Phone: 278-0030
- Victoria Park (between Sheppard and York Mills)
  Phone: 502-2248
- Winston Churchill (at Dundas)
  Phone: 607-0990
- Dufferin (at Steeles)
  Phone: 665-7380
- Newmarket (Yonge and Millard)
  Phone: 830-1815

  *Monday to Friday 9:30 a.m.–9:00 p.m.,
  Saturday 9:30 a.m.–6:00 p.m.
  Visa/MasterCard*
- 57 Spadina Avenue (at King)
  Phone: 585-2052

  *Monday to Saturday 9:30 a.m.–6:00 p.m.
  Visa/MasterCard*

Brand name and designer fashions for men, women, and children at 20%–60% off regular retail prices. Sweaters, sleep wear, gloves, hats, hosiery, shirts, coats, and lots more.

Casual Wear

Athletic Knit Factory Outlet

- 2 Scarlett Road (off St. Clair, north of Dundas)
  Phone: 769-5149

  *Tuesday to Saturday 10:00 a.m.–5:00 p.m.
  Visa/MasterCard*

Up to 70% off suggested retail on casual wear, fleece tops and bottoms in 100% cotton.

Athletic Sports Show

- Unit 17, 2395 Cawthra Road (Q.E.W. and Cawthra)
  Phone: 272-0813

  Monday to Saturday 8:00 a.m.–5:00 p.m.
  Visa/MasterCard

  Outlet for athletic wear, aerobics wear, outer wear, and swimwear. All available for men, women, and children at significant savings.

Clews Clothing Outlet

- 155 Queen Street E., Port Credit (south of Q.E.W. off Highway 2 in Port Credit)
  Phone: 271-0830

  Tuesday to Friday 10:00 a.m.–5:30 p.m.,
  Saturday 11:00 a.m.–4:00 p.m.
  Visa/MasterCard

  Manufacturer's outlet selling men's and ladies' casual clothing—dresses, skirts, blouses, jackets, and trousers in 100% silk, cotton, and linen at up to 50% off regular retail.

Cotton Ginny and Cotton Ginny Plus

- Dixie Value Mall, 1250 South Service Road, Mississauga (Q.E.W. and South Dixie Road)
  Phone: 271-7143

  Monday to Friday 9:30 a.m.–9:00 p.m.,
  Saturday 9:30 a.m.–6:00 p.m.
  Visa/MasterCard/Amex

  Ladies' cotton casual wear—T-shirts, sweat

pants, and sweat shirts at up to 50% off. Inventory includes end-of-lines from other stores plus some special purchases.

Factory Sports Outlet

* 115 Orfus Road (north of Lawrence and west of Dufferin)
  Phone: 256-2808

  Saturday 10:00 a.m.–3:00 p.m.

Savings of 10%–50% on sweat pants and shirts plus running shorts and other active wear.

Golden Mile International Garment Ltd.

* Unit 9, 245 West Beaver Creek Road (Highway 7 and Highway 404)
  Phone: 882-8168

  Monday to Saturday 10:00 a.m.–6:00 p.m.
  Visa/MasterCard

"Harvest Almanac" and "Jasperino" active wear. Down ski jackets and parkas plus knits, cotton shirts, and pants.

Hamper's Clearance Centre

* 1536 Midland Avenue (north of Lawrence)
  Phone: 751-1303

  Monday to Thursday 10:30 a.m.–8:00 p.m.,
  Friday 10:00 a.m.–9:00 p.m.,
  Saturday 10:00 a.m.–6:00 p.m.
  Visa/MasterCard

Men's, ladies', and children's jeans including GWG, Levi's, Calvin Klein, Lee, and Wrangler.

Also shirts, sweat suits, and T-shirts at savings of up to 50%.

Jantzen Factory Outlet

- 966 Dundas Street East, Mississauga (Dundas and Tomken)
  Phone: 272-3841

  Monday to Saturday 10:00 a.m.–6:00 p.m.
  Visa/MasterCard

  Save up to 50% on men's and women's swimwear and casual wear.

Roots

- Upper Canada Mall, Newmarket (Highway 11 and Highway 9)
  Phone: 836-9555

  Monday to Saturday 9:30 a.m.–9:30 p.m.
  Visa/MasterCard

  Clearance centre for Roots stores in Toronto area—jackets, sweat shirts, and shoes. Also carries regular inventory.

Leather Clothing

Canadiana Leather Factory Outlet

- 2869 Dundas Street W. (Dundas, west of Keele)
  Phone: 767-9067

  Monday to Saturday 9:00 a.m.–6:00 p.m.
  Visa/MasterCard/Amex

  Leather clothing for men and women—jackets, skirts, pants, and coats.

Danier Leather Factory Outlet

* 365 Weston Road (north of St. Clair and
  south of Rogers Road)
  Phone: 762-6631

  Monday to Saturday (10:00 a.m.–6:00 p.m.)
  Visa/MasterCard/Amex

Designer samples, slightly imperfects,
end-of-season leather fashions for men and
women at savings of up to 70%.

In Leather

* 109 Orfus Road (north of Lawrence and west
  of Dufferin)
  Phone: 785-1510

  Monday to Saturday 10:00 a.m.–9:00 p.m.
  Visa/MasterCard

Leather and suede jackets and coats at savings
of up to 70%.

Leatherama Inc.

* 7400 Victoria Park Avenue (north of Steeles
  at Steelcase)
  Phone: 479-5066

  Monday to Friday 9:00 a.m.–8:00 p.m.,
  Saturday 10:00 a.m.–6:00 p.m.
  Visa/MasterCard

Savings of up to 60% on men's and ladies'
leather pants, jackets, and skirts.

Children's Clothing

Diaper Factory Outlet

- 1140 Sheppard Avenue W. (west of Dufferin)
  Phone: 631-7776

  Monday to Friday 10:00 a.m.–6:00 p.m.,
  Saturday 10:00 a.m.–5:00 p.m.
  Visa/MasterCard

  Savings of 30%–50% on all sizes of diapers.
  Some children's clothing as well.

Joe-Jo Fashions

- 885 Caledonia (south of Lawrence)
  Phone: 787-1421

  Saturday 9:00 a.m.–12:00 p.m.
  Cash

  Direct-from-the-manufacturer children's
  clothing.

Kids 'N' Co

- 1117 Finch Avenue W. (Finch, between
  Dufferin and Keele)
  Phone: 665-9131

  Monday to Friday 9:30 a.m.–9:00 p.m.,
  Saturday 10:00 a.m.–6:00 p.m.
  Visa/MasterCard

  From 20%–60% off children's clothing.

Kids World Warehouse Store

- 2460 Tedio Street, Mississauga (west of
  Cawthra off The Queensway)
  Phone: 272-4801

Monday to Friday 10:00 a.m.–9:00 p.m.,
Saturday 9:00 a.m.–6:00 p.m.
Visa/MasterCard

Discounts of 40%–60% off brand name
children's clothing including Klub Krickets,
London Fog, Scout Tex, Trimfit, Fox, and many
more.

Peanut Power

- 20 Maud Street (east of Bathurst off
  Adelaide)
  Phone: 361-0200

  Monday to Saturday 10:00 a.m.–3:00 p.m.
  Visa/MasterCard

From 50%–80% off end-of-lines and over runs.
Regular inventory also available.

Petite Palette

- 1185 King Street W. (east of Dufferin)
  Phone: 588-4808

  Monday to Wednesday 10:00 a.m.–6:00 p.m.,
  Thursday 10:00 a.m.–9:00 p.m., Friday 10:00
  a.m.–6:00 p.m., Saturday 10:00 a.m.–5:00
  p.m.
  Visa/MasterCard

50% off regular retail price on cotton children's
clothing (6 months to 9 years).

Sample of the Month Club

- 28 Dufflaw Road (north off Lawrence and
  west of Dufferin)
  Phone: 783-3301

Monday to Thursday 8:30 a.m.–4:30 p.m.,
Friday 8:30 a.m.–4:00 p.m.
Visa/MasterCard

Clothing from size 12 months to adult at discounted prices.

Snugabye Factory Outlet

*   53 Bakersfield Road (Dufferin and Dupont)
    Phone: 531-3297

    Tuesday to Saturday 10:00 a.m.–5:00 p.m.
    Visa/MasterCard

Snugabye brand children's and infant wear, sleep wear, play wear, and underwear. Also infants' bedding, comforters, and cloth diapers.

Hosiery

Bellissimo Pantyhose Distributor's Clearance

*   Unit 13, 136 Winges Road, Woodbridge (Highway 7 between Weston Road and Whitmore)
    Phone: 851-9929

    Monday to Friday 9:00 a.m.–5:00 p.m.,
    Saturday 9:30 a.m.–3:00 p.m.
    Cash

At least 20% off brand name pantyhose including Secret, Cover Girl, and Wonderbra. Also men's cotton socks and some lingerie.

Legs Beautiful Warehouse Store

* Unit 20, 1875 Leslie Street (Leslie and York Mills)
  Phone: 449-7444

  Monday to Saturday 9:00 a.m.–5:30 p.m.
  Visa/MasterCard

  At least 25% off brand name pantyhose and socks.

McGregor Socks Factory Store

* 30 Spadina Avenue (Spadina and Wellington)
  Phone: 979-6760

  Monday to Saturday 10:00 a.m.–5:00 p.m.
  Visa/MasterCard

  From 40%–50% savings on men's and ladies' socks.

Phantom Industries Outlet Store

* 605 Rogers Road (at Keele)
  Phone: 652-6256

  Monday to Wednesday 10:00 a.m.–6:00 p.m.,
  Thursday/Friday 10:00 a.m.–9:00 p.m.,
  Saturday 10:00 a.m.–6:00 p.m.
  Visa/MasterCard

  Pantyhose, body stockings, and swimsuits up to 60% below regular retail. Regular inventory plus seconds.

A C C E S S O R I E S

Corjo Designs

* Unit 13, 361 Steelcase Road W. (off
  Woodbine, north of Steeles)
  Phone: 470-6820

  *Monday to Friday 9:00 a.m.–5:00 p.m.,
  Saturday 10:00 a.m.–5:00 p.m.
  Visa/MasterCard*

Discontinued lines and samples of costume
jewelry.

Yu Fashion Discount Outlet

* 550 Champagne Drive (east of Keele and
  north of Sheppard)
  Phone: 631-9008

  *Monday/Friday 9:00 a.m.–6:00 p.m.,
  Tuesday/Wednesday/Thursday
  9:00 a.m.–5:00 p.m., Saturday 10:00
  a.m.–5:00 p.m.
  Visa/MasterCard*

Costume jewelry, gloves, scarves, and belts.

S H O E S

Athlete's World Clearance Centre

* Dixie Value Mall, 1250 South Service Road,
  Mississauga (Q.E.W. and South Dixie Road)
  Phone: 271-0752

Monday to Friday 9:30 a.m.–9:00 p.m.,
Saturday 9:30 a.m.–6:00 p.m.
Visa/MasterCard

Discounts of 20%–50% off
court/tennis/aerobic/jogging/walking shoes from
Reebok, Avia, and Brooks.

Bally Shoe Clearance Outlet

* Dixie Value Mall, 1250 South Service Road,
  Mississauga (Q.E.W. and South Dixie Road)
  Phone: 271-5898

  Monday to Friday 9:30 a.m.–9:00 p.m.,
  Saturday 9:30 a.m.–6:00 p.m.
  Visa/MasterCard/Amex

Ladies', men's, and children's shoes plus purses
at up to 50% off. As these are end-of-lines,
there is a better selection at some times of the
year than at others.

Bocci Shoes

* 1126 Finch Avenue (west of Dufferin)
  Phone: 736-1732

  Monday to Saturday 10:00 a.m.–6:00 p.m.
  Visa/MasterCard

Clearance for retail outlets offering up to 70%
off men's and women's shoes. No children's
shoes.

Calderone Clearance Warehouse

* 12 Upjohn Road (south off York Mills
  between Don Mills and Leslie)
  Phone: 449-0885

Tuesday/Wednesday 11:00 a.m.–6:00 p.m.,
Thursday/Friday 11:00 a.m.–9:00 p.m.,
Saturday 9:00 a.m.–5:00 p.m.
Visa/MasterCard/Amex

From 20%–50% off brand name ladies' and
men's shoes, boots, slippers, and handbags.
Brand names include Pino Carina, 9 West, and
Naturalizer.

Dack's Shoes Factory Outlet

* 595 Tretheway Drive (Jane, north of
  Eglinton)
  Phone: 241-5170

  Monday to Friday 8:30 a.m.–5:00 p.m.,
  Saturday 9:00 a.m.–4:00 p.m.
  Visa/MasterCard

Men's shoes only.

Ingeborg Shoe Warehouse

* 1681 Finfar Court, Mississauga (south of
  Q.E.W. and east of Winston Churchill)
  Phone: 823-7415

  Monday to Saturday 9:00 a.m.–5:00 p.m.
  Visa/MasterCard/Amex

Clarks, Wallabees, and K Shoes for men and
women at 30%–50% off. Also handbags and
leather jackets.

Joe Singer Shoes Ltd.

* 903 Bloor Street W. (near Ossington)
  Phone: 533-3559

* 1530 Danforth Avenue (near Coxwell)
  Phone: 461-6045

- 10165 Yonge Street (Richmond Hill)
  Phone: 884-0360

  Monday to Wednesday 9:30 a.m.–6:00 p.m.,
  Thursday/Friday 9:30 a.m.–7:00 p.m.,
  Saturday 9:30 a.m.–6:00 p.m.
  Visa/MasterCard

30%–50% off brand name shoes, boots, and
purses. Bally, Florsheim, and Clarks.

Lori's Shoe Manufacturing Outlet

- 99 River Street (east of Parliament between
  Queen and Dundas)
  Phone: 366-7046

  Monday to Friday 8:00 a.m.–5:30 p.m.,
  Saturday 8:30 a.m.–4:00 p.m.
  Cash

Casual shoes and boots direct from the
manufacturer.

Reebok Warehouse Outlet

- Bayview Avenue, north of Aurora Side Road
  (on west side)
  Phone: 727-0704

  Tuesday/Wednesday 11:00 a.m.–6:00 p.m.,
  Thursday/Friday 11:00 a.m.–7:00 p.m.,
  Saturday 9:00 a.m.–3:00 p.m.
  Visa

Discounts of 30% off on current styles and up
to 50% off on discontinued lines and samples of
Reebok and Rockport.

Town Shoes Clearance Centre

* Lawrence Plaza (Lawrence and Bathhurst)
  Phone: 787-5136

* Dixie Value Mall, 1250 South Service Road,
  Mississauga (Q.E.W. and South Dixie Road)
  Phone: 274-3861

  Monday to Friday 9:30 a.m.–9:00 p.m.,
  Saturday 9:30 a.m.–6:00 p.m.
  Visa/MasterCard

Clearance centres for Town Shoes stores in
Metro area. Up to 50% off on ladies' and men's
shoes, boots, and bags. Brand names include
Liz Claiborne and Bandolino. Also carry
regular inventory at retail prices.

Varda Shoes

* 604 Gordon Baker Road (Victoria Park and
  Steeles)
  Phone: 497-3214

  Monday to Saturday 10:00 a.m.–5:00 p.m.
  Visa/MasterCard

Up to 40% off regular items and more off
clearance items. Inventory includes Spanish
and Italian leather shoes and boots.

SPORTSWEAR AND EQUIPMENT

Collegiate Sports Outlet

* Dixie Value Mall, 1250 South Service Road,
  Mississauga (Q.E.W. and South Dixie Road)
  Phone: 274-3471

Monday to Friday 9:30 a.m.–9:00 p.m.,
Saturday 9:30 a.m.–6:00 p.m.
Visa/MasterCard/Amex

End-of-lines of sports equipment such as skis,
ski boots, tennis and squash rackets. Also
men's and women's sportswear and athletic
footwear.

National Sports Centre Clearance Warehouse

* 699 Kingston Road (Highway 401 and
  Whites Road in Pickering)
  Phone: 831-6360

  Monday to Friday 10:00 a.m.–10:00 p.m.,
  Saturday 9:00 a.m.–8:00 p.m.
  Visa/MasterCard/Amex

Clearance centre for sports equipment such as
hockey sticks, skates, exercise bikes, and much
more.

Riordan Ski and Sports Warehouse Showroom

* 1300 Alness (Steeles, west of Dufferin)
  Phone: 738-5533

  Monday to Friday 9:00 a.m.–9:00 p.m.,
  Saturday 9:00 a.m.–6:00 p.m.

Far West, Vuarnet, and Pedigree sports
clothing for men, women, and children at up to
70% off. Brand name skis and boots also
available.

L U G G A G E

Evex Luggage Centre

- 3450 Semenyk Court, Mississauga (west of
  Mavis, south of Central Parkway W.)
  Phone: 277-5911

  *Monday to Friday, 9:00 a.m.–6:00 p.m.,
  Thursday 9:00 a.m.–8:00 p.m., Saturday
  9:00 a.m.–5:00 p.m.*

- 355 Spadina Avenue (south of College)
  Phone: 977-1776

  *Monday to Friday 9:00 a.m.–6:00 p.m.,
  Saturday 9:00 a.m.–5:00 p.m.*

- 180 Steeles Avenue W. (west of Yonge)
  Phone: 881-9161

  *Monday to Wednesday 9:00 a.m.–6:00 p.m.,
  Thursday 9:00 a.m.–9:00 p.m., Friday 9:00
  a.m.–7:00 p.m., Saturday 9:00 a.m.–6:00 p.m.
  Visa/MasterCard*

Up to 50% off suggested retail on brand name
luggage made by Samsonite, Renwick, Skyway,
and many more.

F A B R I C S

B. B. Bargoons Warehouse Outlet

- 230 Denison Street W. (north of Steeles off
  Woodbine)
  Phone: 475-2292

  Monday to Wednesday 9:30 a.m.–6:00 p.m.,

Thursday/Friday 9:30 a.m.–9:00 p.m.,
Saturday 9:30 a.m.–5:00 p.m.
Visa/MasterCard/Amex

One-of-a-kind, ends-of-lines, and remnants
plus special purchases of designer and
decorator fabrics. Also wallpaper.

Designer Fabric Outlet

- 1360 Queen Street W. (at Dufferin)
  Phone: 531-2810

  Monday to Wednesday 9:30 a.m.–6:00 p.m.,
  Thursday/Friday 9:30 a.m.–9:00 p.m.,
  Saturday 9:30 a.m.–6:30 p.m.
  Visa/MasterCard

Discounts of 50% below retail on designer
fabrics. Specializes in silks and tapestries.

Fabric Solution

- 499 Parliament Street (Parliament and
  Carlton)
  Phone: 944-2172

  Monday to Saturday 10:00 a.m.–5:30 p.m.,
  Thursday 10:00 a.m.–8:00 p.m.
  Visa/MasterCard

Up to 80% off fabrics and trims for drapes,
furniture, and other interior design.

HOUSE DECORATION

Architectural Ornament

- 216 Rivermede Road, Unit 6 (Highway 7 and
  Keele)
  Phone: 738-9459

Monday to Friday 10:00 a.m.–4:00 p.m.
Visa

Savings of up to 50% on cornice mouldings, ceiling medallions, exterior mouldings, and trim.

International Paints

- 2045 Drew Avenue, Mississauga (Dixie and Derry Road)
  Phone: 671-0924

  Monday to Friday 8:00 a.m.–4:30 p.m.
  Visa/MasterCard

Save up to 35% on indoor and outdoor paint.

F U R N I T U R E

The Barn

- 1675 Lakeshore Road W. (between Erin Mills Parkway and Mississauga Road)
  Phone: 822-6574

  Monday to Sunday 10:00 a.m.–5:00 p.m.
  Visa/MasterCard

Antique and reproduction furniture—china cabinets, wardrobes, chairs, tables, and antique oil lamps.

De Boers Warehouse Clearance Centre

- 275 Drumlin Circle (Steeles and Keele)
  Phone: 669-1958

  Tuesday to Saturday 10:00 a.m.–5:00 p.m.
  Visa/MasterCard

Floor samples and end-of-lines from stores.

Executive Furniture Rentals

• 48 Samor Road (south of Lawrence)
  Phone: 787-0647

  Saturday 10:00 a.m.–12:00 p.m.
  Cash

  Up to 70% off rental furniture on which the
  lease has expired. Includes sofa beds, coffee
  makers, desks, and chairs. Phone and check
  what is in inventory before driving over.

Grand Furniture Centre

• 7881 Keele Street (north of Highway 7)
  Phone: 650-5914

  Monday to Friday 10:00 a.m.–9:00 p.m.,
  Saturday 10:00 a.m.–6:00 p.m.
  Visa/MasterCard

  Clearance centre for furniture manufacturers.
  Mostly scratched, dented, and discontinued
  lines.

ManuRattan Crafts Co. Ltd.

• 1272 Eglinton Avenue E., Mississauga
  (Dixie and Eglinton)
  Phone: 238-8850

  Monday to Wednesday 10:00 a.m.–6:00 p.m.,
  Thursday/Friday 10:00 a.m.–9:00 p.m.,
  Saturday 10:00 a.m.–6:00 p.m.
  Visa/MasterCard

  Savings of 50%–80% on rattan furniture,
  basketware, hampers, bathroom accessories,
  and more.

Canadian Wholesale Bedding and Bath

- 200 West Beaver Creek Road, Unit 15 (north of Highway 7, west of Leslie)
  Phone: 886-8816

  Monday to Friday 11:00 a.m.–8:00 p.m.,
  Saturday 10:00 a.m.–6:00 p.m.
  Visa/MasterCard

Sheets, duvets, duvet covers, towels, and bath robes. Brand names such as Springmaid. All are available at savings ranging from 30% off retail.

Canalite

- Unit 8, 52 West Beaver Creek Road (north of Highway 7, west of Leslie)
  Phone: 886-6737

  Monday to Wednesday 9:30 a.m.–6:00 p.m.,
  Thursday/Friday 9:30 a.m.–7:00 p.m.,
  Saturday 9:30 a.m.–5:00 p.m.
  Visa/MasterCard

Springmaid and Cannon bedding ensembles plus towels.

Deblins Warehouse Outlet

- 3220 Dufferin Street, Unit 5 (Dufferin and Orfus)
  Phone: 789-2196

Monday to Friday 9:30 a.m.–6:00 p.m.,
Saturday 9:30 a.m.–5:00 p.m.
Visa/MasterCard

Discounted sheets, towels, and table linens.

Eastern Textiles Ltd.

* 164 Bentworth Avenue (3 blocks north of
  Lawrence off Caledonia)
  Phone: 783-1119

  Monday to Friday 8:30 a.m.–4:30 p.m.,
  Saturday 9:00 a.m.–1:00 p.m.
  Cash/Cheques

Texmade sheets, Qualofill duvets, pillows,
Caldwell towels, and shower curtains at
30%–60% savings.

Hardie Factory Outlet

* 970 Verbena Road, Mississauga (north of
  Highway 401, east of Highway 410)
  Phone: 564-2186

  Monday to Friday 8:30 a.m.–4:30 p.m.
  Visa/MasterCard

Outlet store of suppliers of institutional bed
linen and table linen. Savings to be had on
heavy duty bedsheets, towels, and blankets.

Linen Warehouse Clearance Centre

* 1264 Eglinton Avenue E., Mississauga (west
  of Dixie)
  Phone: 602-5629

  Wednesday/Saturday 10:00 a.m.–5:00 p.m.,
  Thursday/Friday 10:00 a.m.–9:00 p.m.
  Visa/MasterCard

Towels, shams, sheets, duvets, and table linen.
All brand names.

Upper Canada Soap and Candle Makers

- 1510 Caterpillar Road, Mississauga (north of The Queensway, east of Dixie Road)
Phone: 897-1710

  Monday to Friday 10:00 a.m.–5:00 p.m.
  Visa

From 50%–70% off soaps, towels, candles, baby clothes, and gift baskets.

KITCHENWARE

Cassidy's Ltd.

- 95 Eastside Drive (north of Queen, east of Highway 427)
Phone: 231-1222

  Monday to Friday 9:00 a.m.–5:00 p.m.
  Visa

High quality, commercial cookware and kitchenware from supplier to hotels and restaurants. Discontinued and clearance items.

Corning Canada Outlet

- 33 West Beaver Creek (north of Highway 7, west of Highway 404)
Phone: 771-3500

  Monday to Saturday 9:30 a.m.–5:00 p.m.
  Visa/MasterCard

Corelle, Revere, and Pyrex dishes, casseroles, and cookware at 20%–50% off retail for seconds and discontinued lines.

FOOD / HOUSEHOLD PRODUCTS

Atlantic Packaging Outlet

* 55 Milliken Boulevard (north of Finch, 1 block east of Kennedy)
  Phone: 298-5343

  Tuesday 9:00 a.m.–2:00 p.m.
  Cash

Bathroom tissue and kitchen towels at significant savings. Check for availability of diapers.

Billy Bee Retail Outlet

* 68 Tycos Drive (1 block south of Glencairn, west of Dufferin)
  Phone: 789-4391

  Monday to Friday 8:30 a.m.–5:00 p.m.
  Cash

Many different types of honey at 40%–50% off retail.

Dad's Cookies Outlet

* 370 Progress Avenue (off Brimley, south of Highway 401)
  Phone: 291-3713

  Monday to Friday 8:30 a.m.–4:45 p.m.
  Cash

40%–60% off broken and misshapen cookies.

TOYS AND CRAFTS

D. L. Stevenson

* Unit 1, 489 Brimley Road (south of Eglinton)
  Phone: 261-6189

  *Monday to Friday 8:30 a.m.–5:00 p.m.,
  Saturday 10:00 a.m.–3:00 p.m.
  Visa/MasterCard*

  Save up to 40% on artists' supplies—brushes
  and canvasses as well as oil, acrylic, and water
  colour paints.

Irwin Toys Ltd.

* 43 Hanna Avenue (between Bathurst and
  Dufferin, south of King)
  Phone: 533-3521

  *Monday to Friday 9:00 a.m.–4:00 p.m.
  Visa/MasterCard*

  Close-outs, ends-of-lines, samples, slightly
  soiled and damaged children's toys. Open all
  year round. In December there is an annual
  warehouse sale with even greater savings.

Lynrich Arts

* 73 Doncaster Avenue (north of Steeles, east
  of Yonge)
  Phone: 771-0411

  *Monday to Friday 9:00 a.m.–6:00 p.m.,
  Saturday 10:00 a.m.–6:00 p.m.
  Visa/MasterCard*

  Art supplies, fabric paints, craft items, and gifts.

Packaging Warehouse Outlet

- 880 Steeprock Drive (Dufferin and Finch)
  Phone: 631-6444

  Monday to Friday 9:00 a.m.–5:00 p.m.,
  Saturday 10:30 a.m.–5:00 p.m.
  Visa

Gift bags, boxes, wrap, ribbon, and tissue sold
in bulk at great savings.

Party Packagers

- 1225 Finch Avenue W. (west of Allen Road
  north)
  Phone: 631-7688

  Monday to Friday 9:30 a.m.–9:00 p.m.,
  Saturday 9:30 a.m.–6:00 p.m.
  Visa/MasterCard

Brand name children's toys such as Milton
Bradley, Hasbro, and Mattel sold at discounted
prices (15%–85%). Further savings on "red
sticker" items. To be eligible, register and also
receive advance mailings of sales.

Sandylion Sticker Designs

- 61 Amber Street (west of Warden, north of
  Denison)
  Phone: 475-6771

  Monday to Friday 9:00 a.m.–5:00 p.m.,
  Saturday 9:00 a.m.–3:00 p.m.
  Cash

Seconds and discontinued stickers, sticker
albums, invitations, and cards. All stickers sold
by the pound.

Young Canada Wholesale Warehouses

- 5171 Steeles Avenue W. (west of Highway 400 between Weston and Islington)
  Phone: 748-8866

- 1990 Ellesmere Road (south of Highway 401 between Markham and McCowan)
  Phone: 438-8880

  Monday to Friday 9:30 a.m.–9:00 p.m.,
  Saturday 9:30 a.m.–5:30 p.m.
  Visa/MasterCard

Complete line of toys and games, trophies, and adult gifts at savings of up to 75%.

ELECTRICAL GOODS

CD Plus

- 1050 Brock Road (south of Highway 401)
  Phone: 837-1816

  Monday to Wednesday, 10:00 a.m.–8:00 p.m.,
  Thursday/Friday 10:00 a.m.–9:00 p.m.,
  Saturday 10:00 a.m.–6:00 p.m.

- 1825 Dundas Street E., Mississauga (west of Highway 427)
  Phone: 629-9255

  Monday to Wednesday 10:00 a.m.–7:00 p.m.,
  Thursday/Friday 10:00 a.m.–9:00 p.m.,
  Saturday 10:00 a.m.–6:00 p.m.
  Visa/MasterCard

CDs and cassettes at prices below regular retail.

Radio Shack Clearance Centre

- 2349 Finch Avenue W. (Weston and Finch)
  Phone: 741-5163

  Monday to Saturday 9:00 a.m.–6:00 p.m.
  Visa/MasterCard/Amex

Clearance centre for Radio Shack stores. Significantly reduced prices on damaged electronics, end-of-lines, and excess inventory—stereos, phones, computer systems, etc.

Sunbeam Factory Outlet

- 1040 Islington Avenue (south of Bloor)
  Phone: 233-3291

  Monday to Friday 9:00 a.m.–5:00 p.m.,
  Saturday 9:00 a.m.–3:00 p.m.
  Visa/MasterCard

From 10%–50% savings on factory seconds, over-runs, and end-of-lines of mixers, blenders, toasters, gas barbeques, and more.

M I S C E L L A N E O U S

Canadian Home Shopping Club

- 605 Rogers Road (Rogers Road and Keele)
  Phone: 658-4725

  Tuesday to Saturday 10:00 a.m.–6:00 p.m.,
  Friday 10:00 a.m.–9:00 p.m.
  Visa/MasterCard

From 10%–50% off items offered on the Canadian Home Shopping Club T.V. network.

Consolidated Salvage Co.

* 2446 Carnforth Road, Units 1 & 2,
  Mississauga (Carnforth, north of The
  Queensway)
  Phone: 276-4230

  Monday to Friday 9:00 a.m.–4:30 p.m.
  Cash

Merchandise from insurance claims. Phone and
check first as merchandise changes every day.

Liquidationworld

* 122 Cartwright Avenue (west of Dufferin
  and south of Highway 401)
  Phone: 787-7200

  Monday to Wednesday 10:00 a.m.–6:00 p.m.,
  Thursday/Friday 10:00 a.m.–9:00 p.m.,
  Saturday 10:00 a.m.–5:00 p.m.
  Visa/MasterCard

Stock changes as different businesses go into
bankruptcy. Merchandise can be as varied as
paint, toys, clothing, and hardware. Phone and
check before going.

Listing of Clearance Centres and Manufacturers' Outlets by Geographic Area

WEST OF THE HUMBER
(including Mississauga)

Electrical Goods

Miscellaneous

N O R T H W E S T
(including Downsview and Concord)

Menswear

Ladieswear

Ladies' and Men's Clothing

Children's Clothing

W E S T   C E N T R A L

Menswear

Ladieswear

Ladies' and Men's Clothing

Casual Wear

Leather Clothing

Children's Clothing

D O W N T O W N

Fabrics

E A S T C E N T R A L

Ladieswear

Ladies' and Men's Clothing

Hosiery

Shoes

E A S T
(including Scarborough and Pickering)

N O R T H
(including Markham, Richmond Hill, and Newmarket)

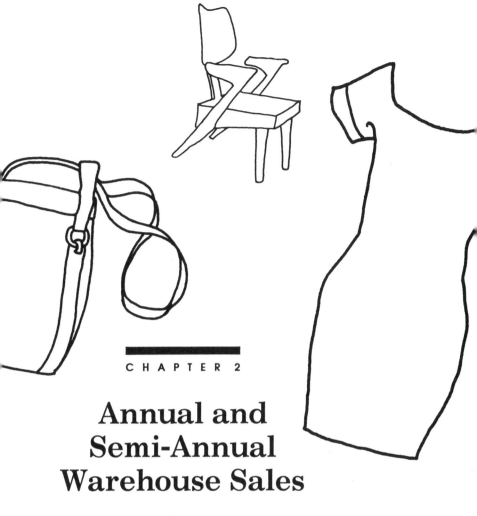

CHAPTER 2

Annual and Semi-Annual Warehouse Sales

Although the outlets listed in Chapter 1 can be gold mines of good deals, the dedicated bargain hunter knows that the semi-annual or annual warehouse event provides the best savings. The Ashleys' warehouse sale is probably the best known of these events. If you are like me, you know that Ashleys have an annual sale, but you aren't sure when it takes place. This section is designed to prevent missing one of these events. Arranged by month it lists sales as they took place in 1991. In most cases, if a business held a successful sale in 1991 they will continue to have annual sales events in the future.

These sales do not always take place in the company's own warehouse. In fact, it is not unusual for a sale to move from one location to another while in progress. Therefore, I have not listed addressses for companies that hold their annual sales away from their own premises, but have provided head office phone numbers so that dates, locations, and payment particulars can be confirmed. If a sale is planned in the near future, the receptionist is sure to know the details.

Be prepared for few facilities at these sales. The changing rooms, if available, will be communal, curtained-off areas. Check whether charge cards will be accepted. Avoid weekends, lunch hours, and evenings, if you can. Know the average retail price for the item you wish to buy and, most of all, be prepared to rummage.

Calendar of Events

J A N U A R Y

Ritchie Super Sale
- Phone: 362-2349

Visa/MasterCard

Annual sale of wedding gowns featuring one-of-a-kind samples from designers such as Sposabella, Bridalane, David Rea, and more. Also available are manufacturers' clearouts at up to 80% off. Location of sale moves according to space available.

F E B R U A R Y

Florence Lewis
- 1230 Sheppard Avenue W., Units 12 & 13 (west of Dufferin) Phone: 633-4494

Visa/MasterCard

"One day only" sale of women's designer sweaters (Mr. Jax, Irving Samuel, Alfred Sung, and Marcus Allan), pants, skirts, suits, dresses, coats, and blazers at 60%–75% off. Held twice a year (February and July) to clean out end-of-season inventory.

Penningtons

* National Distribution Centre, 5101 Orbitor Drive, Mississauga (west of Renforth off Eglinton)
  Phone: 629-3500

  Visa/MasterCard/Amex

Sale is held once a year. Up to 75% off large size ladies' wear (sizes 36–48 and 14–28).

Roots

* Phone: 781-3574

  Cash

Three days only in a specially rented space. Up to 70% off men's, women's, and children's shoes, jackets, sweaters, and handbags.

Serta Manufacturer's Warehouse Clearance

* 37 Bethridge Road (south of Rexdale Boulevard between Martin Grove and Kipling)
  Phone: 743-8241

  Visa

Held twice a year (February and November). Discontinued sofas, chairs, and other furniture.

M A R C H

Beaver Canoe

* 1475 Dupont (1 block west of Lansdowne)
  Phone: 516-0911

  Visa/MasterCard/Amex

  Held three times in 1991 (March, June, and
  December). Up to 75% off shorts, shirts,
  sweaters, and other outerwear.

W. H. Smith Warehouse Book Sale

* 98 Carrier Drive (east of Highway 427, north
  of Finch)
  Phone: 485-6660

  Visa/MasterCard/Amex

  Held twice a year (March and November).
  Major savings on hardcover and paperback
  books for children and adults, Christmas cards,
  and wrapping paper.

M A Y

Bowring Warehouse Sale

* 44 Carnforth Drive (Lawrence, east of
  D.V.P.)
  Phone: 288-9430

  Visa/MasterCard/Amex

  Up to 70% off on tea towels, coffee pots,
  dinnerware, crystal ware, table linens, and
  much more. Sale takes place twice a year

(usually in May and October). Phone and ask to be put on the mailing list.

Canadian Thermos Products Inc.

- 2040 Eglinton Avenue E. (between Birchmount and Warden)
Phone: 757-6231

  Visa/MasterCard

Held in the spring and fall this two-day warehouse sale features picnic coolers and jugs plus vacuum bottles and Thermos jugs.

Dansk Warehouse Sale

- 60 Horner Avenue (south of Evans off Islington)
Phone: 259-1127

  Visa/MasterCard

Three-day sale held twice a year (usually in May and December). Savings of up to 75% on seconds, discontinued lines, special imports, close-outs, samples and experimental dinnerware, cookware, flatware, crystal, and accessories.

Grand Specialities Ltd.

- 650 Barmac Drive (Steeles and Weston)
Phone: 748-3500

  Visa/MasterCard

One-day sale held twice a year (May and December). Includes Lindt chocolates, Chambord jams, Jacksons teas, Amora sauces, Effie Marie cakes, and many more speciality treats.

Harvey Lister's

* 155 Champagne Drive, Unit 8 (south of
  Finch and west of Dufferin)
  Phone: 630-4441

  Visa/MasterCard

Sale of dinnerware, crystal, glass ware, and
cutlery. Includes brand names such as Royal
Doulton and Armani.

Lady Manhattan of Canada

* 1185 Caledonia (near Lawrence and
  Dufferin)
  Phone: 785-4960

  Visa

Held three times a year, always on a Saturday.
Discounts from 50%–75% off on previous
season's blouses and shirts by John Henry,
Lady Manhattan, Above the Crowd, etc.

Laura Secord

* 1500 Birchmount (at Ellesmere)
  Phone: 751-0500

  Cash

One-day sale held in May in 1991. The
advertisements did not mention the Laura
Secord name. Up to 50% savings on Laura
Secord, Black Magic, Quality Street, and Dairy
Box chocolates.

Norma Fashions

* 388 Carlaw (north of Dundas, east of D.V.P.)
  Phone: 469-5346

  Visa/MasterCard

From 50%–80% off ladies' leather jackets,
coats, pants, and skirts. These are
end-of-season lines from stores.

Ports and Tabi Warehouse Sale

- 75 Scarsdale Road (off York Mills, east of
  Leslie)
  Phone: 865-0102 or 443-0502

  Visa/MasterCard/Amex

Held twice a year (May and November).
Combines Ports, Tabi, and Alfred Sung ladies'
dresses and men's suits plus blazers, trousers,
and sweaters.

Tilley Leathergoods

- 10 Canmotor Avenue (east of Islington,
  south of The Queensway)
  Phone: 259-2385

  Visa/MasterCard

From 50%–75% off on wallets, portfolios,
handbags, and attaché cases produced by
Tilley. Also held in November or December.

J U N E

Beaver Canoe

(see March)

Mikasa Warehouse Sale

- 121 McPherson Street (north of Steeles and
  west of Warden)
  Phone: 474-0880

Visa/MasterCard

Up to 80% off on surplus stock, discontinued lines, and samples of dinnerware, flatware, giftware, and crystal.

Revlon Warehouse Sale

* Phone: 276-4500

Warehouse space rented specifically for the sale. Up to 75% off Revlon products.

J U L Y

Florence Lewis

(see February)

Lilycups Inc.

* 2121 Markham Road (Markham and Finch) Phone: 691-2181

Cash

Cups, plates, and containers for picnics or the cottage.

S E P T E M B E R

Eddie Bauer Warehouse Sale

* Phone: 961-2525

Visa/MasterCard/Amex

Location determined closer to the time of sale. Phone for details. At least 50% off on excess stock, discontinued lines, and damaged goods from area Eddie Bauer stores. Includes jackets, coats, boots, shoes, gifts, and men and women's clothing. As the sale progresses the discounts become deeper.

Tilley Endurables

- 900 Don Mills Road (just north of Eglinton)
  Phone: 441-6141

  Visa/MasterCard

Discontinued lines, seconds, and samples at significant savings. Seconds of Tilley hats at half price. Also held at end of December.

O C T O B E R

Bowring Warehouse Sale

(see May)

N O V E M B E R

Alfred Sung

- 720 King Street W., Suite 210 (King and Bathurst)
  Phone: 365-0330

  Visa/MasterCard

Sample, end-of-season, and irregular sweaters, blouses, skirts, and jackets plus fabrics by the metre.

Ashley's Warehouse Sale

- 62 Railside Road (east of D.V.P. and south of Lawrence)
  Phone: 924-2900

  Visa/MasterCard/Amex

  Lasts for two weeks in November, and is supposedly the largest sale of its kind in North America. Major savings on china (Royal Doulton and Wedgewood), glassware, and cutlery. There is some special buying done specifically for this sale which is considered to be the best sales event in Toronto.

Birks Warehouse Sale

- Phone: 449-4011

  Visa/MasterCard

  Birks' first warehouse sale was held in 1991 in a location rented specifically for the sales event. Exceptional discounts were offered on items from local Birks' outlets.

Canadian Thermos Products Inc.

(see May)

Chesebrough-Pond Products Sale

- Phone: 294-9770

  Cash

  Held in 1991 for the first time in three years. The great thing about this sale of cosmetics is that a percentage is donated to charity.

Coles Warehouse Book Sale

- 90 Ronson Drive (Highway 401 and Martin Grove)
  Phone: 243-3132

  Visa/MasterCard

  Hardcover and paperback books for adults and children at discounted prices.

Conair Consumer Products

- 6707 Goreway Drive, Unit 4 (Mississauga, south of Derry Road)
  Phone: 798-1320

  Visa/MasterCard

  At least 50% off Conair products—hair dryers, curling irons, setters.

Harvey Lister's

(see May)

Lewiscraft Warehouse Sale

- 40 Commander Boulevard (south of Huntingwood, west of McCowan)
  Phone: 291-8406

  Visa/MasterCard

  Up to 70% off on craft items and 20% off catalogue goods.

Lipton's International Ltd.

- 29 Connell Court (Kipling and Evans)
  Phone: 251-3121

  Visa/MasterCard/Amex

Lipton's and Heritage House sale on ladies' clothing. Phone to be put on the mailing list for the dates of the next sale.

Mikasa Warehouse Sale

(see June)

Mollie Gladstone Accessories

• 441 Esna Park Drive, Unit 12 (north of Steeles and east of Victoria Park) Phone: 479-3200

Visa/MasterCard/Amex

Savings of up to 70% on high-fashion jewelry and evening bags.

Monique Fashions

• 466 McNicoll Avenue (east of Highway 404, north of Finch) Phone: 491-1094

Visa/MasterCard

Christmas decorations, jewelry boxes, pens, and many other gift items.

Norma Fashions

(see May)

Ports and Tabi Warehouse Sale

(see May)

Rosenthal China

* 55G East Beaver Creek Road (north of Highway 7 near Leslie)
  Phone: 886-2270

  Visa/MasterCard

Discontinued and end-of-line Rosenthal china, stemware, and giftware. Ask to be put on the mailing list for sale times.

Serta Manufacturer's Warehouse Clearance

(see February)

W. H. Smith Warehouse Book Sale

(see March)

D E C E M B E R

Beaver Canoe

(see March)

Braun

* 1025 Tristar Road (Tristar and Tomken, Mississauga)
  Phone: 670-9200

  Visa/MasterCard

Held every December for three days. Up to 50% off blenders, shavers, and many other Braun products.

British Canadian Imports

- 405 Britannia Road E., Unit 19 (Highways 10 and 401 in Mississauga)
  Phone: 890-2344

  Cash

  Imported toiletries and gifts such as potpourri, stationery, and scented drawer-liners which are end-of-lines and discontinued items.

Colonial Designs Manufacturing Inc.

- 70 Production Drive (off Progress, east of McCowan)
  Phone: 289-0509

  Visa

  Up to 80% off jewelry that has all been produced at Colonial.

Dansk Warehouse Sale

  (see May)

Down Under Sportswear

- 572 King Street W., Suite 301
  Phone: 594-0148

  Cash

  Seconds and samples of women's and children's jumpsuits and sweats in prints and fleece.

Gene Natale Warehouse Clearance Sale

- 102 Peter Street (east of Spadina off Front)
  Phone: 593-0505

Visa/MasterCard

Warehouse clearance of end-of-season men's clothing.

Grand Specialities Ltd.

(see May)

Hammet Enterprises Warehouse Sale

- 5250 Finch Avenue E., Unit 6 (between Markham and McCowan)
  Phone: 297-1728

  Visa

Scarves, shawls, and other accessories at up to 70% off retail. This sale is held by a number of importers joining together.

Izod Lacoste Factory Sale

- Second Floor, 1020 Lawrence Avenue W. (at Dufferin)
  Phone: 781-6625

  Visa/MasterCard

Up to 75% off retail on end-of-line, samples, and imperfects of men's and women's sportswear.

Lifestyles Warehouse Sale

- 501 Alden Road (north of Steeles and west of Warden)
  Phone: 946-8320

  Visa/MasterCard/Amex

Originally known as the Pot Pourri sale. Great selection of kitchen goods and household items at up to 70% off retail.

Louise Kool and Galt Ltd.

* 1149 Bellamy Road, Unit 11 (off Progress, west of Markham)
  Phone: 439-4322

  Visa/MasterCard

Educational toys and games by Fisher Price, Lego, and Little Tykes. Held sale for first time in six years in 1991.

Lou Myles

* 14 Jody Avenue (north of Highway 401, east of Highway 400)
  Phone: 743-1767 or 748-1097

  Visa/MasterCard

Two-day sale. Factory clearance of men's suits, shirts, coats, ties, and sweaters.

Mistral Skiwear Clearance

* Phone: 771-1884

  Visa/MasterCard

Sale moves to different locations depending on availability of space. From 60%–80% off on women's and men's ski outfits.

Petrocelle and Woolskins Warehouse Sale

* Phone: 785-1771

  Visa/MasterCard/Amex

Location changes according to space. Men's and ladies' fashions at discounted prices. Leather goods as well as silk shirts and wool suits.

Revlon Warehouse Sale

(see June)

Swedish Comfort Children's Wear Sale

- 132 Atlantic Avenue (Dufferin and King)
  Phone: 531-3530

  Visa

100% cotton children's clothes from newborn to age 14. Three other sales during the year but December is the main one.

Tilley Endurables

(see September)

Tilley Leathergoods

(see May)

Woods Canada Warehouse Sale

- 401 Logan Avenue
  Phone: 465-2403

  Visa/MasterCard

Manufacturer of high quality down-filled products (used by the Canadian Army). From 40%–70% off retail prices on jackets, vests, and parkas.

Alphabetical Listing of Companies Offering Warehouse Sales

- Alfred Sung (*November*)
- Ashley (*November*)
- Beaver Canoe (*March, June, December*)
- Birks (*November*)
- Bowring (*May, October*)
- Braun (*December*)
- British Canadian Imports (*December*)
- Canadian Thermos Products Inc. (*May, November*)
- Chesebrough-Pond (*November*)
- Coles The Book People (*November*)
- Colonial Designs Manufacturing Inc. (*December*)
- Conair Consumer Products (*November*)
- Dansk (*May, December*)
- Down Under Sportswear (*December*)
- Eddie Bauer (*September*)
- Florence Lewis (*February, July*)
- Gene Natale (*December*)
- Grand Specialities Ltd. (*May, December*)
- Hammett Enterprises (*December*)
- Harvey Lister's (*May, November*)
- Izod Lacoste (*December*)
- Lady Manhattan of Canada (*May*)
- Laura Secord (*May*)
- Lewiscraft (*November*)
- Lifestyles (*December*)
- Lilycups (*July*)
- Lipton's International (*November*)

- Louise Kool & Galt Limited (*December*)
- Lou Myles (*December*)
- Mikasa (*June, November*)
- Mistral Skiwear (*December*)
- Mollie Gladstone Accessories (*November*)
- Monique Fashions (*November*)
- Norma (*May, November*)
- Penningtons (*February*)
- Petrocelle and Woolskins (*December*)
- Ports and Tabi (*May, November*)
- Revlon (*June, December*)
- Ritchie (*January*)
- Roots (*February*)
- Rosenthal China (*November*)
- Serta Manufacturers (*February, November*)
- Swedish Comfort Children's Wear/KSM Textiles (*December*)
- Tilley Endurables (*September, December*)
- Tilley Leathergoods (*May, December*)
- W. H. Smith Books (*March, November*)
- Woods Canada Limited (*December*)

SEE APPLICABLE MONTH IN CALENDAR OF EVENTS FOR STORE DETAILS

Other Bargain Shopping Centres

Discount Malls

Canada has been slow to pick up on the popularity of the U.S. Factory Outlet Malls. This is changing now with the success of the Dixie Value Mall leading the way for other such malls in the Toronto area. Some of the stores mentioned in the first chapter of this book are located in these malls. The stores listed individually met my criteria of being true discount outlets, that is, the majority of the stock had been previously offered at a retail price. However, if visiting a discount mall it is worthwhile to check the other stores located there. Use the same principle as before and be aware of the retail price of the items you wish to purchase.

Dixie Value Mall

* 1250 South Service Road, Mississauga (Q.E.W. and South Dixie Road)

  Monday to Friday 9:30 a.m.–9:00 p.m., Saturday 9:30 a.m.–6:00 p.m.

Lawrence Plaza

* Northwest corner of Lawrence and Bathurst

  Monday to Friday 9:30 a.m.–9:00 p.m., Saturday 9:30 a.m.–6:00 p.m.

Rexdale Plaza

* 2267 Islington Avenue (Highway 401 and Islington north)

  Monday to Friday, 10:00 a.m.–9:00 p.m., Saturday 9:30 a.m.–6:00 p.m.

Discount Outlet Areas

Orfus Road

* Between Dufferin and Caledonia, north of Lawrence

Many clothing manufacturers have moved to this area from Spadina. Also has household linen outlets.

Spadina Avenue

- Between Front and College

Although not a mall, this is a great area for fashion stores—both clearance centres and direct-from-the-manufacturer.

Department Store Clearance Centres

The Bay Fashion Clearance Centre

- Dixie Value Mall
  1250 South Service Road, Mississauga
  (Q.E.W. and South Dixie Road)
  Phone: 271-6868

  Visa/MasterCard
  Monday to Friday 9:30 a.m.–9:00 p.m.,
  Saturday 9:30 a.m.–6:00 p.m.

Eaton's Warehouse Store

- 2233 Sheppard Avenue W. (Highway 400
  and Weston Road)
  Phone: 343-2233

  Monday to Friday 9:30 a.m.–9:30 p.m.,
  Saturday 9:30 a.m.–6:00 p.m.

Sears Clearance Centres

- Dixie Value Mall
  1250 South Service Road, Mississauga
  (Q.E.W. and South Dixie Road)
  Phone: 278-6400

- Rexdale and Islington Avenue (opposite Rexdale Plaza, north of Highway 401)
  Phone: 744-4500

- Warden Avenue (Warden, south of Eglinton)
  Phone: 288-7000

  Monday to Friday 10:00 a.m.–9:00 p.m., Saturday 9:30 a.m.–6:00 p.m.

Simpsons Furniture Clearance Centre

- 5601 Steeles Avenue W. (between Weston Road and Islington Avenue)
  Phone: 748-3024

  Monday to Friday 10:00 a.m.–9:00 p.m., Saturday 9:30 a.m.–6:00 p.m.

Warehouse Stores

The increasing popularity of warehouse "super stores" has led to a revolution in retailing. These stores offer discounted prices and no frills but you must be a member to purchase their products.

The Price Club

- 3025 Ridgeway Drive, Mississauga (Dundas and Winston Churchill Boulevard)
  Phone: 820-9300

- 137 Christlea Road (Highway 400 and Highway 7)
  Phone: 744-8173 or 744-8174

  Monday to Saturday 10:00 a.m.–9:00 p.m.

To take out a membership you must show proof that you own your business or work for an organization that is recognized by The Price Club (for instance the government or a chartered bank). Memberships cost $25 plus $10 for each additional member. No credit cards are accepted—just cash and cheques.

Major savings can be found here but some items are sold at retail prices. Therefore it is important that you check prices before shopping.

INDEX

Clearance Centres and Manufacturers' Outlets

Companies Offering Warehouse Sales

Other Bargain Centres

Other Whitecap titles
of special interest to Ontarians:

The Ontario Gardener

The Only Complete Gardening Guide
Written and Illustrated Specifically for
Ontario Gardeners
By Trevor Cole
7 1/2 x 10, 248 pp. $24.95 paperback
40 pages of colour photos
ISBN 1-895099-42-0

A Guide to the Golf Courses of Ontario

By Alan Dawe
6 x 9, 304 pp. $16.95 paperback
ISBN 1-895099-44-7

A Taste of Ontario Country Inns

By David Scott
6 x 9, 224 pp. $14.95 paperback
Line drawings and B & W photos
ISBN 1-895099-95-1

The Ontario Getaway Guide

By David Scott
6 x 9, 224 pp. $16.95 paperback
60 B & W photos
ISBN 1-895099-46-3

52 Weekend Activities for the Toronto Adventurer

By Sue Lebrecht
6 x 9, 208 pp.
$12.95 paperback
52 B & W photos and maps
ISBN 0-921396-26-0

Toronto's Many Faces

*A Guide to the Multi-cultural
Make-up of the City*
By Tony Ruprecht
with Vida Radovanovic
and Gail Hanney
5 1/4 x 9 3/16, 320 pp.
$17.95 paperback
ISBN 0-921396-20-1